A Six-Year-Old's View
of Foster Care, Adoption,
and the Art of Wearing a Cape

By Deanna Roy
and Little Dude

casey shay press

Copyright © 2018 by Deanna Roy
All rights reserved.

No part of this book may be used or reproduced by any means, graphic, electronic, or mechanical, including photocopying, taping, and recording without written permission, except in the case of brief quotations embodied in critical articles and reviews.

Casey Shay Press
PO Box 160116
Austin, TX 78716
www.caseyshaypress.com

Paperback ISBN: 9781938150814

Also available in hardcover.
ISBN: 9781938150807
And as an Ebook: ISBN: 9781938150821

Library of Congress Control Number: Pending

For everyone who has helped
our family along the way.

~ Thank you. ~

Contents

Foreword	7
A Dude's Eye View	11
Cookie Whisperer	12
The Jolly Stalker	13
Spit-Take	14
Turn Off the Shades	15
It Makes Everything Better	16
A Little Dude at Disneyland	17
Dog Eat Dog	18
Caped Cool	19
Tummy Time	20
The Santa Loophole	21
Be Nice to the Ref	22
Almost Sick Day	23
Give It the Boot	24
Still Cute	25
But They're Handy	26
Cash Flow	27
Unrewarding	28
Directional Debut	29
Bowling in the Rain	31
Lint Trap Logic	32
Lint Trap Logic, Part 2	34
If There Be Dragons	35
Cookied into a Corner	36
Helping the Elderly	37
Boy, Interrupting	38
Shadow Priorities	40
Candy Facts	41
Tactful Retaliation	42

Friends on the Flip Side	43
Digestive Conundrums	44
Need No Teef	45
Families and Other Forces of Nature	47
Thanksgiving Digs	48
Christmas Surprises	50
Forever Home	51
A Mom Is Born	53
Misnomers	54
Santa Secrets	55
Broken Ears	56
Monster Dirt	57
Puppy Power	58
Work Trip	60
Reindeer Games	62
Kissing Tree	63
Observation	64
Baby Pictures	65
Bad at Legos	66
Jolly Old St. Mom	68
Not-So-Good Week	69
Lunch Lesson	70
Let Him Eat Cake	71
It's All About the Bat	73
Batman Moon	74
Patient Moon	75
No One Told Batman	76
Capes Are Cool	77
The Only Word That Matters	79
Moon, Revisited	80
The Randomness of Clouds	81
OMGolly	82
Heroes and Orphans	83
About the Authors	84

Foreword

A Word from Little Dude's Mom

The first time I saw Little Dude, my family met him and his current foster mom at a burger shop in North Austin. He'd been out of the hospital for five weeks, and he was silly, curious, and excited. You'd never know that he'd been through more than any little one should have to bear. He'd survived, and with a small child's resilience, he was ready for whatever might be next.

After about a half-hour together, he jumped in our car to spend a few days with us. The caseworker was being cautious with him as his six months in foster care had been the worst-case scenario in every way. They wanted a commitment. After two consecutive weekends, my husband and I agreed we would adopt him, no matter what. So the Department of Family Services moved him in with us.

He was four years old. We were home number six.

He was a cute little thing, full of mysterious ideas and unexpected behavior. He ate anything we gave him, often shoveling food directly into his mouth from the plate. Gifts were overwhelming and created a fear of losing them, so we added toys and books and games slowly.

He spent the first several weeks almost entirely on my lap. I carefully, over time, took him to story time at local libraries and gradually encouraged him to move from facing my chest, to turning outward, to sitting beside me. One of my greatest mom-moments occurred when he jumped up to pass out craft materials to other kids. He finally trusted that I wouldn't just leave him there. This took three months.

Little Dude struggled with what to call us, starting with our first names, then making us Mama and Dada when he needed to refer to us in front of other children, until a sort of break-through when he decided we were the real deal. You'll see these changes reflected in our conversations, and his struggle with his identity inside a new family.

Despite our having raised two biological children to high school already, our lives were turned upside down in every way. So much goofiness, so much hardship, so much to learn. As Little Dude got braver, hiding less and talking more, he clearly wanted to make up for the years he'd spent in chaos. He began showing us his view of the world.

So I started typing up the conversations he had with me, my husband, and my two teen daughters. In this way, friends, family, and acquaintances could get to know him even if they couldn't meet in person. Little Dude needed a lot of people in his corner, and his conversations let the world understand who he was and where he came from. His particular spin on everyday moments have made many people laugh.

Little Dude's story before he arrived at my home is his to tell, not mine. But sharing the journey of how we got to know each other, and how he came to understand what it meant to belong to a family, has become a way to let the world meet him, little by little, conversation by conversation.

With his adoption in 2017, Little Dude officially became a part of our family. I'm pleased to introduce him to you through his own words and his unique spin on the important things in life — family, friends, adoption, bacon, Santa Claus, and most of all — Batman.

Actually, you can ignore all of those things except Batman.

Deanna Roy
November 2018

A Dude's Eye View

Explaining a swallowed tooth to the tooth fairy.

Cookie Whisperer

LD: The check-out lady said there were no more M&M cookies, but she was wrong! [Holds up cookie with triumph.]
Me: Oh, good. That one is your favorite.
LD: I almost had to eat chocolate chip!
Me: But you like chocolate chip too.
LD: Not as much as M&M.
Me: Well, I'm glad she was wrong about the M&M cookies.
LD: You want to know how I found it?
Me: Sure.
LD: It was hidden behind a chocolate-chip one.
Me: So how did you know it was there?
LD: It called to me.
Me: The cookie?
LD: Yes. It said, "Little Dude! Little Dude!"
Me: Wow. Does food call to you often?
LD: Cookies do.
Me: Anything else?
LD: Not broccoli. Broccoli never calls to me.
Me: What if it did?
LD: I'd say, "Nobody's home!"

The Jolly Stalker

LD: Some of the houses on our street don't have Christmas lights.
Me: Some people don't put them up.
LD: How will Santa know to go to their house?
Me: Well, if he knows if you've been naughty or nice, he probably knows where you live.
LD: And he sees you when you're sleeping.
Me: And he knows when you're awake!
LD: That's just creepy.

Spit-Take

LD: What is that horrible green thing you are eating?
Me: A spinach bake.
LD: It looks terrible!
Me: I like spinach.
LD: Spittage is gross. S-P-I-T. See, it has spit in the name!
Me: Actually, it's SPIN-ach. Not spit-age.
LD: Well, it ought to have spit in the name.
Me: Why?
LD: Because I would spit it out!

Turn Off the Shades

LD: It's bright outside.
Me: It's summer!
LD: I need my sunglasses.
Me: They're in your cupholder.
LD: Wow, they work!
Me: They always have.
LD: How do sunglasses work?
Me: They make the sun less bright.
LD: Like when the screen is too bright, and you turn it down so it doesn't hurt your eyes?
Me: Yes. Exactly like that.
LD: [Yanks them off.] That's dangerous!
Me: Why?
LD: If everybody wears them, they could make the sun go out!

It Makes Everything Better

LD: Are you happy this morning?
Me: I am.
LD: Like Sam-I-am?
Me: Was he happy?
LD: Well, he had bacon!
Me: I thought it was ham.
LD: No, it's Green Eggs and Bacon.
Me: I'm pretty sure it's *Green Eggs and Ham*.
LD: [Grumbling.] It *should* be Green Eggs and Bacon.

A Little Dude at Disneyland

Me: Look! There's Winnie the Pooh!
LD: Hey, this rail is wet!
Me: It sure is! Do you want to go over there and see the castle?
LD: [Running hands on rail.] Just let me dry off this rail.
Me: Okay.
...
...
Me: Is it dry yet?
LD: Yeah, but there's another one.
Me: You sure you don't want to get on a ride? See Mickey? Walk around?
LD: I like these wet rails.
Me: Is this the best part? Drying the rails at Disneyland?
LD: Of course! We don't have rails like this at home!

Dog Eat Dog

LD: Are those prairie dogs?
Me: Prairie dogs live outside in holes.
LD: No, on your plate. Prairie dogs.
Me: Which thing are you calling a prairie dog?
LD: That brown round thing.
Me: You mean a hush puppy.
LD: ARE THEY MADE OF PUPPIES?
Me: No, no. It's cornmeal mostly. A yellow flour.
LD: Then why are they called that?
Me: I think people would feed them to the dogs so they'd be quiet while they were cooking out on a hunt.
LD: Well, I'm not going to eat them.
Me: They're pretty good.
LD: It's *dog food*.

Caped Cool

LD: Mama!
Me: What's up?
LD: My cape won't stay on.
Me: Hmm, this blanket is a little thick to tie well.
LD: Can we cut it in a strip?
Me: The blanket? Heavens, no. We can't cut a blanket to make a cape.
LD: Then what do I do?
Me: You have lots of capes in your closet. The one from Six Flags. The magician one.
LD: Those aren't cool!
Me: So real capes aren't cool? Only blanket ones?
LD: Those are too small!
Me: Oh, I see. You need a big blanket cape. Let's see if we can use a safety pin to make it stay.
LD: Okay.
Me: All right, there. You'll have to ask my help to take it off.
LD: Oh, I won't need you.
Me: It's a big pin. You might get poked!
LD: No. It's never coming off.
Me: The cape? Why not?
LD: It'll make me lose my cool!

Tummy Time

LD: Why is my tummy being so mean?
Me: It's sick. Sick tummies are mean.
LD: When I was mean, you made me say I was sorry.
Me: You want me to have your tummy say it is sorry?
LD: You think it would do it?
Me: We could try.
LD: No.
Me: Why not?
LD: I might freak out if my tummy starts talking.

The Santa Loophole

LD: Santa was here!
Me: Looks like it!
LD: He ate all the cookies and drank all the milk!
Me: He sure did.
LD: Good thing Santa isn't lactose intolerant.
Me: We could have given him your special milk.
LD: We should do that next year, just in case one of the elves wants some and *he* is lactose intolerant.
Me: Good idea.
LD: There's stuff in our stockings!
Me: I see that!
LD: I *knew* I wasn't on the naughty list! It was close, though.
Me: You think so?
LD: Honestly, I think it only changed right at the end.
Me: Like the last few days?
LD: Like right before bed. I had a plan this year.
Me: A plan? To get on the nice list?
LD: Yes. Maybe I can't be nice all the time. But I can do it for one night. So I'm nice on Christmas Eve!
Me: Hmm. Maybe you should try to work on it a little more than just one night.
LD: But I'm being like Santa.
Me: I think Santa is nice all year round.
LD: But he only does the hard work for just one night!

Be Nice to the Ref

LD: Why do I get to stay up late?
Me: It's the UT Bowl Game!
LD: I'm gonna watch some FOOTBALL!
Me: We all are! And maybe see your sister on TV for one second if we're lucky.
Eliza: I hope the refs aren't stupid idiots.
LD: Language!
Eliza: Well, they might deserve it!
LD: You can't talk that way about people!
Me: It's sort of a tradition in football to say mean things about the referees when they aren't doing a good job.
Eliza: They are on TV. They can't hear you.
LD: *I* can hear you.

Almost Sick Day

LD: Just so you know, I'm going to have a sick tummy in the morning so I can stay home from school with you.

Me: Hmm. Well, your sister has an appointment tomorrow, so I won't be here.

LD: Okay. I'll be sick the next day instead.

Me: They're having hot dogs in the cafeteria that day.

LD: Never mind.

Give It the Boot

LD: Where did you put the bag?
Dad: In the trunk.
LD: Why do they call it a trunk?
Dad: Because people used to store things in big wood boxes called trunks. They were strapped on the back of the car.
LD: That's terrible. Trunks should be in front!
Dad: Why?
LD: Because elephant trunks are in front!
Dad: Some countries call the trunk the "boot."
LD: Boots go on the bottom!
Dad: Well, that's true for people.
LD: Tires should be boots.
Dad: That actually makes more sense.
LD: And the trunk should be the *butt*.

Still Cute

Me: Time for bath, buddy.
LD: Just one more minute.
Me: What are you doing?
LD: Looking in the mirror.
Me: You've been there for a while.
LD: It takes a while!
Me: What takes a while?
LD: Making sure I'm still cute!

But They're Handy

LD: I got a new library book!

Me: The *Captain Underpants Handbook*. Cool.

LD: It's full of hands!

Me: Is it?

LD: Yeah! See? [Opens book. Flips pages.] Wait. There aren't any hands in here!

Me: Well, generally a handbook just means you hold all the information about something in your hands.

LD: That's just wrong.

Me: I can see how it would be confusing.

LD: *They* are confused. *All* books are handbooks.

Me: I don't think so. Some books just tell stories.

LD: But don't you hold them in your hands when you read them?

Me: Well, yes.

LD: Then they are handbooks.

Cash Flow

LD: What is that a picture of?
Me: A diamond-encrusted car.
LD: How much does it cost?
Me: A million dollars, apparently.
LD: Let's buy it!
Me: I don't have that much money.
LD: I'll buy it!
Me: You don't have that much money.
LD: I have an idea. I'll go do some chores. And you'll pay me money. And then I'll give it to you for the sparkly car.
Me: That would be a lot of chores.
LD: I get a dollar for sweeping the floors!
Me: That's a lot of floors.
LD: I'd do it for a sparkly car!
Me: But if I pay you the money, then you're just giving me money I gave to you. I still have the same amount of money.
LD: But I worked and gave it to you!
Me: But it came from me!
LD: No, it came from me working.
Me: But I paid it to you from my money.
LD: But I gave it back to you.
Me: Well, okay. This isn't working. I'm not sure we need a sparkly car anyway.
LD: Of course we do!
Me: What if the diamonds fall off?
LD: Then we'll sell them.
Me: For what?
LD: To buy the sparkly car!

Unrewarding

LD: So Dada, Mama said you won an award. Are you getting a big trophy?

Dad: Nope.

LD: A medal?

Dad: Nope, just a piece of paper.

LD: That's it? Are you going to hang it in your office?

Dad: Well, not my actual office, but in the lobby.

LD: So no trophy, no medal, and you don't even get to keep the paper yourself?

Dad: That's right.

LD: Well, that's not much of an award.

Directional Debut

LD: So today I had to learn where we live.
Me: You mean our city?
LD: No, the numbers and the word.
Me: Oh, our address.
LD: Yeah, that.
Me: So what is it?
LD: [Random string of numbers that do not resemble ours.]
Me: Hmm. That wasn't quite it.
LD: Well, I know how to get there, though.
Me: Okay, why don't you show me how to walk home? You lead.
LD: Okay!
Me: So which way do we go on this street?
LD: To the right!
Me: Okay. Lead the way!
LD: When you get to the crossing guard, you have to *stop* until she says *go*.
Me: Got it.
LD: Now, *stop*!
CG: Good job, sir!
LD: I'm showing Mama how to get home.
Me: Now where?
LD: Straight!
Me: Over the fence?
LD: No!
Me: Under the fence?
LD: Silly Mama.
Me: Should I crash *through* the fence like the Hulk?
LD: Please stop talking about fences.
Me: Okay.

LD: So up here, we have to cross the street.
Me: Now? Without looking?
LD: *No*! You'll get smooshed like a pancake!
Me: But I like pancakes!
LD: Mama, are you taking this seriously?
Me: I'll do better.
LD: Okay. Look both ways. And *stop* for cars.
Me: Got it.
LD: See, we made it without getting smooshed like pancakes.
Me: We did! You're good at this!
LD: Let me get out my invisible map. See this street on the map?
Me: How did you learn to read invisible maps?
LD: Oh, I just figured it out.
Me: By yourself?
LD: Well, yeah! The map says we have to crunch these leaves.
Me: The map says it?
LD: Actually, you always say it. We should crunch the leaves.
Me: I do say that.
LD: Louder! Stomp the leaves!
Me: Doing it!
LD: Can you see our house now?
Me: I do! You got me home!
LD: I told you I could do it.
Me: With your invisible map?
LD: You really need to get one of those.

Bowling in the Rain

LD: Thunder is the scariest sound!
Me: You think so?
LD: I know so! Listen to it!
Me: You know what I've heard about it?
LD: No.
Me: It's actually God bowling. That big crash is when the pins fall down.
LD: I like bowling!
Me: I know! I guess God likes it too.
LD: Do you think that story is true?
Me: I don't know. I can't see up there.
LD: You think he just got a strike?
Me: Maybe!
LD: I bet it was just a spare.
Me: It was a lot of pins falling, that's for sure.
LD: Are you just telling me this story to make me feel better?
Me: Is it working?
LD: Yeah. You can tell me stories like that any time you want.

...

LD: Remember when you told me thunder was God bowling?
Me: I do.
LD: What does it mean when it rains then?
Me: Some people say the angels are crying.
LD: I don't think so.
Me: Oh?
LD: It's God crying. Because he's losing at bowling.

Lint Trap Logic

LD: Mama! Mama!
Me: What is it, baby?
LD: Can I check the lint in the dryer?
Me: Wait. What did you say?
LD: The lint! On that little screen you take out of the door of the dryer!
Me: What about it?
LD: Can I check it?
Me: Um. Okay. Sure. Go ahead.
LD: Yay! [Takes off for garage.]

...

LD: Mama! Mama!
Me: Did you find the lint trap?
LD: It was dirty! There was lint in it!
Me: Yeah, I normally take it out before I start it the next time.
LD: Can I take it out?
Me: Well, okay. Sure.
LD: Yay! [Back to garage.]

...

LD: Mama!
Me: Yes, baby.
LD: I cleaned it *all* out. All of it.
Me: Did you throw it away?
LD: Yes.
Me: What made you want to get the lint out?
LD: Because it was dirty!
Me: But *why* did you want to get the lint out?

LD: [Exasperated.] Because it was dirty!
Me: But why *now*?
LD: [Holding his head.] BECAUSE IT WAS DIRTY!

Lint Trap Logic, Part 2

LD: I have to clean my room!
Me: Are you ready for school?
LD: Yes! Breakfast! Dressed! Tied my own shoes!
Me: All right. You can clean your room.
LD: [Madly putting toys in box and clearing floor, which was actually pretty clean.]
Me: Nice job, buddy.
LD: I had to get it all clean!
Me: Are you expecting somebody?
LD: No.
Me: Then why did you have to clean it?
LD: Because it was messy!
Me: But why did you have to clean it right *now*?
LD: Because it was messy!

If There Be Dragons

Little Dude at the Renaissance Faire.

Man selling dragon's teeth necklaces:
:	This will protect you from dragons!
LD:	Cool. [Slips it over his head.]
Man:	Do you want it?
LD:	Naw. [Takes it off.]
Man:	But now you aren't protected from dragons!
LD:	I don't need it.
Man:	Sure you do! To keep the dragons away.
LD:	I hate to say it, but I have to. [Puts hand on man's arm.] Dragons aren't real.

Cooked into a Corner

LD: Mama?
Me: Yes, baby.
LD: Do you serve me a healthy breakfast?
Me: It's healthy enough.
LD: Is it healthy like dinner?
Me: Um, no, you eat more at dinner. But it's okay.
LD: But is it healthy *enough* like dinner?
Me: Yes. I take care of you. Don't worry.
LD: Well, you said I could have dessert if I eat a healthy dinner.
Me: That's right.
LD: So, if I eat all my healthy *breakfast*, can I have a Girl Scout cookie?
Me: Sorry, buddy, dessert is for healthy dinner.
LD: Okay.
...
LD: Mama?
Me: Yes, baby?
LD: Can I have a Girl Scout Cookie *for* breakfast?
Me: Sorry, baby. Not healthy.
LD: Mama?
Me: Yes, baby?
LD: Are donuts healthy?
Me: [Sigh.] No, not really.
LD: But you sometimes let me have *those* for breakfast.
Me: Only every once in a while.
LD: So, can I have a Girl Scout cookie for breakfast every once in a while?

Helping the Elderly

LD: I can cross this street all by myself.
Me: I bet you could. But I need someone to help ME, so I need you to walk with me.
LD: Well, okay.
[We cross.]
LD: So, this *next* one, I can do by myself.
Me: But I still need your help.
LD: Let me teach you so you can do it. You stop. You look right, left, right. And if nobody's coming, you go. Walk, don't run.
Me: I think I remember teaching *you* that.
LD: Well, you must have forgot.
Me: Why do you say that?
LD: Because you can't cross the street without me! You forgot how!
Me: Well, maybe it's because it makes me nervous. I need someone with me.
LD: I know why you won't let me cross by myself.
Me: Because I'm nervous?
LD: I think you've gotten old, and you can't remember things anymore.
Me: Uh...
LD: Here, I'll hold your hand across the street. It's okay that you're old. I don't mind.

Boy, Interrupting

LD: Hey Mama!

Me: I need to finish my instructions to Elizabeth, and then I'll talk to you. Okay?

LD: So when you are talking to someone else, I have to wait my turn?

Me: That's right. [Finishes sentence.] Okay, what did you need?

LD:

Me: Did you still have a question?

LD: [Whispering.] Someone's talking on the radio.

Me: It's okay to interrupt the radio.

LD: Okay, so I can talk when someone on the radio is talking, but not someone in the car?

Me: That's right. Unless a person in the car says, "Can you wait a moment? I need to hear this."

LD: So if a person in the car says a person on the radio is more important, then the radio becomes a person in the car.

Me: Exactly.

LD: How do you know when the person on the radio is done? The radio never stops!

Me: The person who was listening will let you know they are ready to listen to you.

LD: But the radio keeps going even when we're talking.

Me: We don't really listen to it when we're talking to each other. Sometimes I turn it down.

LD: Good thing you don't turn ME down.

Me: That's why you learn how to speak politely. So no one has to ask you to turn yourself down.

LD: This is too hard. I want to be the radio.

Shadow Priorities

LD: I feel bad for my shadow.
Me: Why?
LD: I keep stepping on it!
Me: It doesn't hurt it. That's just what shadows do.
LD: Well, I can run away from my shadow.
Me: Really? I'd like to see that.
LD: [Takes off and comes back.] Hey, it's as fast as I am!
Me: That's fast.
LD: Yeah. You think it's faster than me?
Me: I guess you can ask it for a race.
LD: Shadow! I'll race you! Go! [Takes off again.]
Me: That looked like a tie.
LD: How do I make it go away?
Me: Your shadow?
LD: Yeah! I can make it run, walk, and jump. But I can't make it go away.
Me: You want me to tell you how?
LD: Yes!
Me: Run to that tree over there, and your shadow will go away before you reach it.
LD: Really?
Me: Try it.
LD: [Takes off to the shade of the tree.] It's gone!
Me: I told you.
LD: How do you know everything?
Me: Oh, I definitely don't know everything.
LD: Well, you know all the important stuff.

Candy Facts

LD: This Snickers package is wrong.

Me: Really? Why?

LD: It should just be Snicker. Because there is only one candy bar in it.

Me: I think the name refers to something else. Yes, see here, it's named for a horse. That's why it has the S at the end.

LD: Nope.

Me: Why the nope? It says right here. Named for a horse.

LD: It's still just one candy bar. If they want to call it *Snickers*, they have to put *two* in there.

Tactful Retaliation

LD: Where are you going while I'm at school, Mama?

Me: To get my hair cut.

LD: But you have a great hair cut already!

Me: Well, thank you. But sometimes I want to make it different.

LD: What are you going to do to it?

Me: Maybe I'll shave it all off.

LD: That will look terrible!

Me: Well, it might. But you should never tell someone their hair looks terrible.

LD: What if it does?

Me: Then maybe you shouldn't mention it.

LD: What if she asks?

Me: Mention something else. Remember in the movie *Up* when the dog got distracted? They would say SQUIRREL?

LD: Yes! So if your hair looks terrible, I should say SQUIRREL!

Me: Now you've got the idea.

LD: [Considering my morning hair.] SQUIRREL!

Friends on the Flip Side

LD: Where did you go?
Me: I went to a coffee shop.
LD: Was anybody else there?
Me: Some of my friends. Can you guess who?
LD: Was Henry there?
Me: Yes. He was.
LD: Oh. My. Goodness.
Me: That's pretty special, huh?
LD: Well, yeah!
Me: Who else do you think was there?
LD: Irma?
Me: No, not this time.
LD: Well, that's a bummer.
Me: It's always a bummer without Irma.
LD: Was Ivy there?
Me: She was!
LD: She always holds me upside down by my feet!
Me: Yes, she likes that.
LD: Did she hold *you* upside down by your feet too?
Me: Not this time.
LD: Bummer. Why does she do that to me?
Me: Because you're cute.
LD: I am pretty cute. Especially upside down.

Digestive Conundrums

LD: I have a problem.
Me: What is that?
LD: I burped.
Me: I noticed.
LD: But I had a problem!
Me: What was the problem?
LD: When I burp I'm supposed to say, "Excuse me!"
Me: That's right.
LD: But I'm not supposed to talk with my mouth full!
Me: Also right.
LD: So what do I do when I burp with my mouth full?
Me: Sigh.
LD: I told you it was a problem.

Need No Teef

LD: My mouth feels funny!
Me: Losing your two front teeth at the same time will do that.
LD: [Spots a jogger.] LOOK AT MY TEEF!
[Jogger nods but keeps going.]
LD: She didn't look.
Me: She's busy running.
LD: Okay. [Spots an older kid coming up behind us.] LOOK AT MY TEEF!
[Kid looks at him like he's crazy and hurries on past.]
LD: He didn't look either.
Me: Well, not everyone is interested in teeth. You don't have to try to stop everyone. Okay?
LD: Okay. [Spots a parent.] LOOK AT MY TEEF!
[Parent smiles indulgently as she passes.]
LD: She only pretended to look.
Me: She did. Maybe we won't show every single person?
LD: Okay. Nobody cares.
Me: Your friends will care. You can show them.
LD: Okay.
[Spots another parent and child, doesn't mention his teeth.]
LD: But Mama?
Me: Yes, baby.
LD: How do I know who to show my teef?

Me: Well, you have friends, right?
LD: But what if those people *could* be my friends? How will I know if I don't show them my teef?
Me: That's a very good point.
LD: I know. I will show them my teef. The nice people will look. They are my friends.
Me: That's actually a good idea. Show everyone your teeth.
LD: See, I know some things.
Me: Yes, you do. You really do.

Families and Other Forces of Nature

Thanksgiving Digs

LD: I don't understand Thanksgiving.
Me: It's a day you give thanks for what you have.
LD: Like Legos?
Me: Legos sound good.
LD: I'm thankful for my sisters.
Me: That's good too.
LD: Not just Emily and Elizabeth.
Me: Okay.
LD: My other sisters too.
Me: They are very special.
LD: My brothers too.
Me: They are good brothers.
LD: I wish I saw them more.
Me: We will do our best to see them as often as we can.
LD: What are you thankful for?
Me: For Emily. For Elizabeth. For Kurt. And for you.
LD: Me?
Me: Yes, you.
LD: But I'm lots of trouble.
Me: It's the best kind of trouble.
LD: Deanna?
Me: Yes, baby.
LD: If I am too much trouble, will I go away? Like before? At the other places?
Me: Nope. We are going to adopt you. As soon as [our caseworker] says we can.

LD: I don't know what that means.
Me: It means you live here forever and ever.
LD: Here? With you and Kurt?
Me: Yes. With me and Kurt.
LD: Well, that's weird.
Me: Why is that weird?
LD: Because this house is kind of small for three kids.

Christmas Surprises

LD: Thank you for the Ninja Turtle hat! I really like it!
Me: You're welcome.
LD: And the Legos.
Me: Of course.
LD: And the Paw Patrol game.
Me: You're welcome!
LD: How did you know what I wanted?
Me: You told us!
LD: You were listening?
Me: Of course!
LD: Nobody ever did that.
Me: Well, we do.
LD: Thank you for listening.
Me: Thank you for being our little boy.

Forever Home

LD: After I'm adopted, can I come back here and live?

Me: Being adopted means you stay here forever and ever. You don't need to come back, because you are already here.

LD: So I can't come back?

Me: You can come back. Any time you leave, you can come back.

LD: So I'm not getting adopted?

Me: Let's start over. What do you think adoption means?

LD: That I don't get to go home.

Me: Well, you won't go back to your old home.

LD: But this is my home. So I don't get to go back here?

Me: Okay. Let's try this a different way. Adoption means you get to change your name to Kurt's. You want to practice saying it?

LD: [Random Consonants that are roughly Kurt's.]

Me: Good!

LD: Why can't I be Roy?

Me: Kurt is excited that you will have his name.

LD: Can I be [Random Consonants]-Roy?

Me: Sure. But that's a lot to spell!

LD: That's what I want. When I'm adopted. Both!

Me: And you know you are staying here, right?
LD: Forever and *ever*!
Me: Until you get married.
LD: Nope. I'm not getting married. I'm going to live here forever.

A Mom Is Born

LD: Mama!

Kurt: [Snapping awake.] Did he just call you Mama?

Me: I think so. I've been upgraded. [Heads to room.]

LD: I had a nightmare.

Me: I'm sorry, baby. Do you want something?

LD: I just wanted you.

Misnomers

LD: So can I ask you something?
Me: Always.
LD: Should I call you Mama all the time?
Me: That's up to you. You can call me Deanna if you like that better.
LD: I like both things.
Me: Then you can call me both things. You usually say Mama in front of your friends.
LD: Yeah, definitely.
Me: Why is that?
LD: Because one time my friend Luke called his mom Amanda and he got grounded!

Santa Secrets

LD: Deanna, I mean Mama, should I write a letter to Santa?
Me: Sure. What do you want to say?
LD: I don't want to tell you.
Me: Hmmm. That's sort of hard since you don't know all your letters yet.
LD: I can try.
Me: Absolutely. You know where the paper is.
LD: Okay. [Gets paper and scribbles random letters.]
LD: I have a question.
Me: What's that?
LD: How do you spell brother?
Me: B-r-o-t-h-e-r
LD: How do you make H?
Me: Like this.
LD: How do you spell sister?
Me: S-i-s-t-e-r
LD: Okay. How about safe?
Me: S-a-f-e
LD: Okay. I'm done. Can I mail it?
Me: Sure. Here's an envelope. Seal it up tight.
LD: Did you look?
Me: Nope, I don't have a clue what you wrote.

Broken Ears

Me: So what happened in PE today?
LD: Well...my ears broke.
Me: Really? How so?
LD: They turned off.
Me: Like a light switch?
LD: YES. Just like that. Off on off on.
Me: So what happened while your ears were *off*?
LD: The teacher told us not to roll the ball into the bowling pins.
Me: And so what did you do?
LD: I rolled the ball into the bowling pins.
Me: When did your ears switch back on?
LD: When she said I was in trouble for rolling the ball.
Me: You want to just take responsibility for what you did instead of blaming it on your ears?
LD: Okay, Mama.
Me: You have to listen in class.
LD: Okay, Mama. But I think Dada's ears break too.
Me: Really? When?
LD: When you said the trash needed to go out.

Monster Dirt

Me: So what can we do to help you when you feel out of control at school?

LD: Not make me do anything hard so I don't get frustrated?

Me: Well, some days things that are usually easy, *seem* hard.

LD: I know, I'm going to take the little monster out of my head and flush him down the toilet.

Me: Okay.

LD: The monster in my head is the problem.

Me: Sounds like something to try.

LD: [Pulls imaginary tiny monster out of his hair and holds it out.] I'm going to flush it now.

Me: Okay.

LD: [Walks to the bathroom, then actually flushes the toilet.] I'm going to wash my hands! [Turns on water.]

Me: Do you really need to wash your hands after that?

LD: I touched a monster! Wouldn't you?

Puppy Power

Me: So we met with your teacher yesterday.
LD: Uh oh.
Me: She sends me emails, you know.
LD: Uh oh.
Me: She told us about the dog incident.
LD: You mean with Harley?
Me: No, not our dog.
LD: What dog?
Me: The dog at school.
LD: There's no dog at school.
Me: The stuffed animal dog.
LD: Oh.
Me: You know the one?
LD: Yeah.
Me: And you know what you did with it?
LD: I don't remember.
Me: I think you do. Does *pew pew* ring a bell?
LD: Uh, maybe.
Me: *Pew pew* out his butt?
LD: I might remember that.
Me: *Pew pew* out his butt at your classmates?
LD: Come on, that's funny.
Me: Your teacher didn't think it was funny.
LD: She laughed!
Me: She wasn't laughing at the conference.
LD: Okay, Mama.

Me: I can't believe I'm having to say this, but it is not appropriate to lift the tails of stuffed dogs and have them *pew pew* like they are shooting poop at your classmates.
LD: Okay, Mama.
Me: You won't do that again?
LD: No, Mama.
Me: You promise?
LD: What if it's a cat?

Work Trip

LD: Dada's been gone a long time.
Me: I know. I miss him too. He'll be back tonight, though.
LD: He's never been gone this long before.
Me: Well, he tried very hard to avoid having to go on long work trips until now.
LD: I don't like it.
Me: I don't either. But we're still together.
LD: I think you're wrong.
Me: What about?
LD: About Dada coming home.
Me: What did he say on the phone last night?
LD: That he was coming home tomorrow.
Me: Do you think that wasn't true?
LD: People always say that.
Me: What do they say?
LD: That they are coming back. It's bad.
Me: Why is that bad?
LD: Because they don't come back. I know these things.
Me: You do know these things. And you are very brave. And very strong. And you know what I think?
LD: What?

Me: I think you are going to find out that in this house, things are different. That people do come back. And that it's okay for Mom or Dad to go away for a little while, or even a long while, because we will always come back.
LD: Okay. But Mama?
Me: What, baby?
LD: I probably won't believe you until he comes back.

Reindeer Games

LD: It's dark! We have to spread out the reindeer food!

Me: It's okay. You have time. We haven't even had dinner yet.

LD: But I have to get it out there! [Grabs the bag of oats and runs for the door.]

Me: Okay. Wait up.

LD: I have to spread it all around. They can't miss it!

Me: Why is this so important? We didn't feed them last year.

LD: Well...it's because of the naughty list.

Me: Santa's list?

LD: Yeah. That one.

Me: You worried you're on it?

LD: [Tossing oats.] Well...I've been a little bit naughty and a little bit nice.

Me: What does feeding the reindeer have to do with Santa's list?

LD: Well...if the reindeer stop to eat, maybe Santa will fill my stocking while he's here.

Me: Even if you're on the naughty list?

LD: I might be on it a little bit.

Me: Well, for the record, I don't think you're on it.

LD: I'm still feeding the reindeer.

Kissing Tree

Me: I'm going to tell you a story.

LD: Is it a long story? Because I really want that light-up flying toy.

Me: It's an important story.

LD: Okaaaay.

Me: When your dad and I first knew each other and had met together a few times, we came here to this giant lighted tree.

LD: Really? Like a long time ago?

Me: Yes, a long time ago. Eleven years now.

LD: Did you buy light-up flying toys?

Me: No. But right here under this tree, right where we're standing, your dad kissed me for the first time.

LD: That's gross.

Me: It wasn't gross.

LD: It's gross.

Me: I guess you probably want that flying toy now.

LD: Yes. And please don't tell me any more gross stories.

Observation

LD: What did you and Dada eat while I was at camp?

Me: I had a sandwich with mushrooms, zucchini, and red peppers.

LD: But you don't like red peppers!

Me: I don't mind them in a sandwich.

LD: Did they burn your mouth?

Me: Nope. Red peppers aren't hot.

LD: Well, you don't like jalapeños, because they are too spicy. And you don't like green peppers because they taste weird to you. But Dada DOES like jalapeños, and he DOES like peppers, even the funny green ones that come with pizza.

Me: Wow. You really remember—

LD: And you and Dada both like onions but Dada likes olives and you don't. Except that one kind in a black can.

Me: Okay! Anything else?

LD: I'll remember you like red peppers in a sandwich.

Me: Sounds good. But why is that important?

LD: Because *you* are important.

Baby Pictures

LD: Look at that picture of Peppa Pig as a baby! [Laugh snorts at the TV.]
Me: She was a very tiny pig.
LD: Was I a very tiny baby?
Me: I bet you were!
LD: Can you show me some of *my* baby pictures like Peppa Pig?
Me: Oh. Gosh. I have one from when you were three.
LD: Where are my baby pictures?
Me: I'm not really sure.
LD: Oh. Right. I didn't live here.
Me: You arrived when you were four.
LD: I forgot.
Me: Maybe we can draw some pictures?
LD: But I don't know what I looked like! You don't either!
Me: I think we could do a pretty good job anyway.
LD: That's true. Just draw the cutest baby in the world!

Bad at Legos

LD: I'm sorry I yelled at you.
Me: You were in the red zone, huh?
LD: Yeah.
Me: Do you remember what you called me?
LD: No.
Me: Let's think about it together. Do you remember kicking the table? Slamming the door to your room? Moving the furniture in front of it so we couldn't get in?
LD: I remember I couldn't do my Legos.
Me: That's what started it. What's the last thing you remember?
LD: Hiding under the table.
Me: Yes, you did that after you refused to take a deep breath or do a wall pushup or any of your calm-down strategies.
LD: That always works!
Me: Not this time. You were really, really red.
LD: But I'm good at Legos!
Me: You are. But this time they got to you. Do you know why this time?
LD: I don't know.
Me: It's okay that you don't know. Sometimes when we're upset, it takes us back to other times we were upset. So we act like it's the old times, not the new time.
LD: I don't want to talk about old times.
Me: That's okay. You don't have to.
LD: What did I call you?

Me: Stupid. You said I was stupid, this house was stupid, and everyone in the house was stupid.
LD: I'm sorry, Mama.
Me: We're okay. We're here to help. You know what?
LD: What?
Me: I still love you even when you call me stupid.
LD: You always say that. Every time.
Me: Because it's true. Every time.

Jolly Old St. Mom

LD: So, are you Santa?
Me: Did someone at school tell you I was?
LD: No.
Me: Then why are you asking?
LD: Can you just tell me? I really need to know.
Me: Well, I do buy you gifts. I wrapped them last year, remember?
LD: But the ones in my stocking. And on the fireplace.
Me: I can definitely say I didn't wrap those.
LD: So it's a little bit of you, and a little bit of Santa?
Me: That sounds like a good way to think of it.
LD: So, where's your naughty list?

Not-So-Good Week

LD: So, I guess the principal called you.
Me: Yup.
LD: So, I guess she told you everything that happened.
Me: Yup.
LD: So, I guess I'm grounded again.
Me: Yup.
LD: I'll start packing my toys.
Me: Good plan.
LD: I can still read books, though, right?
Me: Yes. And do art. And puzzles.
LD: It's been a while since I watched TV.
Me: Yeah, screens went away a couple days ago. I thought you would have them back by now.
LD: I'm not having a good week, am I?
Me: No, not really.
LD: You know what I said to myself while I waited for you to pick me up?
Me: Hmmm. Did you practice apologies to your classmates?
LD: No.
Me: What did you say to yourself?
LD: What you always tell me to say.
Me: Which part?
LD: The one I say every night. In my head.
Me: What's that?
LD: Tomorrow is a new day.

Lunch Lesson

LD: You came to lunch at school with me!
Me: Yes, I am here.
LD: You brought McDonalds!
Me: Also true.
LD: [Opening Happy Meal box]. And there's a toy!
Me: A popular part of every Happy Meal.
LD: But you never go to McDonalds!
Me: Ah, but this isn't about me.
LD: [Closes box.] I didn't earn this.
Me: Lunch with Mom and McDonalds isn't something you earn.
LD: But I got in a lot of trouble at school yesterday.
Me: That you did.
LD: And you were really upset.
Me: Yes, I was.
LD: So why did you bring me lunch when I was in the most trouble?
Me: Because it's when you're in the most trouble that you need your Mama to bring you lunch the most.

Let Him Eat Cake

Me: So are you excited about tomorrow?
LD: I'm a little happy and a little sad.
Me: What's the happy part?
LD: I'm happy I'm getting adopted tomorrow.
Me: I'm happy too. What's the sad part?
LD: It's a little scary. I get sad when I'm scared.
Me: What is scary about tomorrow?
LD: I've never been to court before.
Me: You want to know a little secret?
LD: I *love* secrets.
Me: I know. Here's mine. I'm a little scared too.
LD: You? You're the mom! You can't be scared.
Me: Well, it's true.
LD: What are you scared of?
Me: We're meeting people we've never met before.
LD: Well, I'll be there.
Me: That's right! You will!
LD: And Dada. And Emily. And Elizabeth.
Me: All true. We'll know lots of people!
LD: So you don't need to be scared, Mama.
Me: I think you're right. I won't be scared if you are there. Will you still be scared if I am there?
LD: No. I won't be scared. Well, as long as you do something.
Me: What's that?

LD: Even though I'm going to be a first grader, can I hold your hand?
Me: I would be very happy to hold your hand.
LD: Okay. Then I'll just be happy then.
Me: Good.
LD: Of course, there's another way I'll for sure be happy.
Me: What's that?
LD: If we had cake.

It's All About the Bat

Batman Moon

With his sister Elizabeth.

Eliza: Look at the super moon! It's so big!
LD: No it's not! I could hold it in my hand!
Eliza: It's only small because it's far away. It's a super moon because it's closer than usual.
LD: I don't see a *cape*. It's not a super anything.
Eliza: Sigh.
LD: Can it be a Batman moon instead?

Patient Moon

LD: I love you!
Me: I love you too!
LD: I love you bigger than the whole wide world, to the moon and back.
Me: I --
LD: Wait.
Me: What?
LD: I just love you the whole wide world.
Me: Why is that?
LD: I don't want to go to the moon anymore.
Me: Why not?
LD: Is it still a super moon?
Me: Maybe a little.
LD: Well, I'm waiting for a Batman moon.

No One Told Batman

LD: Does Batman have birthdays?
Me: Hmm. I guess so. Everybody has birthdays.
LD: I had a birthday once.
Me: You've had several birthdays.
LD: How many birthdays has Batman had?
Me: I'm not really sure. He's been around a long time. 60?
LD: That's a lot of candles!
Me: It is.
LD: That could blow up his face!
Me: Probably not.
LD: You're right. Nothing gets to Batman.
Me: Because he's a superhero?
LD: No, silly Mama. Because he's not real!

Capes Are Cool

LD: I don't know what to be for Halloween.
Me: I thought the choice was obvious.
LD: You mean Batman?
Me: Of course.
LD: I thought I'd try something new.
Me: Nice. What ideas do you have?
LD: Darth Vader.
Me: Bold choice, since Darth Vader is a bad guy.
LD: What?
Me: Darth Vader is the villain. He has a Death Star. He blew up a planet.
LD: But Death Stars are cool!
Me: I don't think the people on the planet thought so.
LD: It's just a story.
Me: That's true. Stories aren't real.
LD: So Darth Vader didn't really do anything bad. Not in real life.
Me: You have me there.
LD: You know what makes Batman and Darth Vader so cool?
Me: Hmm. The way they wear black or really dark gray?
LD: You're silly, Mama. Anybody can wear black.
Me: Their masks?
LD: No.

Me: Their gravelly voices? [Channeling Christian Bale.] I'm Batman.
LD: Don't ever do that again.
Me: Ha, okay. But is it that?
LD: No.
Me: So tell me. What is it about Batman and Darth Vader that makes them so cool?
LD: Their capes.

The Only Word That Matters

LD: B-b-b. A-a-a.

Me: Watcha doing?

LD: I'm concentrating, Mama! B-b-b. A-a-a. T-t-t. BAT!

Me: Okay.

LD: M-m-m. A-a-a. N-n-n. Man! Batman!

Me: Good job, reading, buddy! What else does that box say?

LD: I'm done.

Me: There's nothing else on the box?

LD: No, I'm done learning to read.

Me: Really? There's a lot more in the world to read other than Batman.

LD: Nothing else is important.

Moon, Revisited

LD: I love you, Mama.
Me: I love you too.
LD: I love you to the Batman moon and back.
Me: Batman has been your favorite a long time.
LD: Actually, no.
Me: No?
LD: I love you to the Batman and Wonder Woman moon and back.
Me: Oh, Wonder Woman too? Did you want a boy and a girl?
LD: No. I just wanted more heroes.

The Randomness of Clouds

LD: Do you see something in the clouds?
Me: Nope.
LD: I see an elephant.
Me: Ah, okay. Sure. An elephant.
LD: No, actually, it's a plane with no wings.
Me: Okay. That works too.
LD: I guess that would make it a boat.
Me: Sure.
LD: Why is a boat flying in the sky?
Me: Didn't you say it was a cloud?
LD: Oh yeah. It's a cloud boat flying in the sky.
Me: That's nice.
LD: I wish it had Batman in it.
Me: That's random.
LD: Batman is never random.

OMGolly

LD: Mom, what does OMG mean?
Me: It means you're surprised.
LD: I thought it stood for something.
Me: It does. You take the first letter of the words "oh my gosh" and say them instead. O for oh. M for my. G for gosh.
LD: Isn't it easier just to say "oh my gosh"?
Me: Well, it's less to type on your phone.
LD: Oh. I don't have a phone.
Me: It will make more sense when you do.
LD: I thought it stood for something else.
Me: Oh?
LD: Oh my God.
Me: Hmm, yes, it stands for that, too. But some people don't like using God that way, so they say gosh.
LD: Do you say gosh?
Me: Generally, yes.
LD: I'm going to say OMB. That way nobody gets upset.
Me: That's sounds like a good idea. What does it stand for?
LD: Oh my Batman!
Me: Why Batman?
LD: Batman is full of surprises.

Heroes and Orphans

LD: Can we read one more page?

Me: One more. Let's see, it says, "Zane had been an orphan all his life."

LD: That's sad! He doesn't have any parents!

Me: That is sad.

LD: Good thing I have parents!

Me: Good thing we have you!

LD: You know, Batman doesn't have parents either. Or Robin!

Me: I think you'll often find in stories about heroes, they lost their parents at a young age.

LD: Good thing I never lost my parents!

Me: But…well. Okay.

LD: What's wrong?

Me: You're…you know…gosh. Is that how you feel?

LD: You'll be with me forever and ever, right, Mom?

Me: We will. Of course we will.

LD: See! I don't have to worry. I won't ever be just like Batman.

About the Authors

Little Dude goes to elementary school, plays soccer, rides his green bike, and considers himself a Lego Master Builder. When he's not being Batman.

Deanna Roy is the six-time *USA Today* bestselling author of women's fiction and books for kids. She lives in Texas with her husband, three kids, a puppy dog, a kitty, and six oversized goldfish.

Join Deanna's email or text list for updates on new releases at www.deannaroy.com.

www.ingramcontent.com/pod-product-compliance
Lightning Source LLC
Chambersburg PA
CBHW071325040426
42444CB00009B/2085